1

1 Introduction

The 2007–09 financial crisis raised awareness of the potentially destabilizing effects of financial intermediaries' reliance on wholesale funding. The increased complexity and interconnectedness of the financial system have changed how intermediaries finance themselves and how their liquidity can come into question. In particular, many financial firms finance their positions through repurchase agreements (repos), which are secured loans backed by financial assets. In the context of repos, destabilizing bank runs can manifest themselves through an increase in haircuts, where the cash borrower receives less money for the same collateral, forcing it to finance its position with internal funds. Alternatively, bank runs can be triggered by a lender's refusal to roll over the repo altogether, implying an abrupt withdrawal of funding.

Despite the considerable literature that emerged on how repo markets developed during the crisis, the empirical evidence is not conclusive on how bank runs evolved. On the one hand, Gorton and Metrick (2012) show a dramatic increase in haircuts during the crisis, effectively forcing borrowers to use more of their own assets to finance their existing positions or to risk selling off parts of their portfolios at fire sale prices. On the other hand, Krishnamurthy et al. (2014) show only a mild variation in margins. They also document that collateral classes, such as private label Asset-Backed Securities (ABS), which did see a reduction in financing seemed to have lost it precipitously.

This paper reconciles these two empirical facts with a stylized model of repo seen from the perspective of a financial intermediary bringing together initial cash lenders with ultimate cash borrowers. The difference in margins between these repo contracts implies a cash surplus for intermediaries, effectively giving them a *liquidity windfall* through repo rehypothecation.

More specifically, this paper models dealers as intermediating funds between competitive cash lenders — money market funds (MMF) — and prime brokerage clients — hedge funds (HF) — through repos and reverse repos respectively. Hedge funds use the loan to finance the purchase of the repo's underlying collateral, and dealers use the same collateral to finance the hedge fund's repo. The two lending contracts are determined endogenously and their terms of trade depend on a dealer's need for liquidity and each contracts' resolution in bankruptcy. In modeling dealers' liquidity needs I assume they have a preference for cash in the initial leg of the loan. That is, a positive cash inflow is more valuable initially than on the final debt payment. The notion is that an influx of liquidity can allow dealers to finance other activities or give them flexibility to supplant any liquidity shortfalls. When modeling dealers' default risk, I assume they can default for reasons unrelated to their role as cash intermediaries, which counterparties price accordingly. The resolution of the repo and reverse repo in default plays an important role in deciding the equilibrium terms of trade. Specifically, counterparties' reduced ability to access unsecured claims on the dealer pins down the interest rate/haircut tradeoff. [1]

The resulting equilibrium predicts a higher haircut for the cash borrower than for the cash lender, implying a windfall of funds for the dealer on the initial leg of the loan. The dealer has free rein to use this surplus of cash. Given cash lenders' limited recourse to the dealer's assets upon default, they set the repurchase price (final debt payment) to equal the asset's worst case outcome, in effect insulating them from the dealer's counterparty risk. This suggests that there are relatively stable contracting conditions between dealers and cash lenders. On the other hand, the hedge fund suffers a loss if the dealer defaults, as it loses the asset altogether, effectively forfeiting the initial margin used to purchase it. Given that in equilibrium the cash lender is insulated from the dealer through the repo's collateral, and the cash borrower has an unsecured claim on the dealer in case of default, the cash borrower has incentives to withdraw its asset from the dealer if its solvency comes into question. Thus, a run does not ensue because of the cash provider's unwillingness to lend but because of the collateral provider's unwillingness to borrow — that is, to deliver the initial collateral. The model also shows that whenever the correlation between the dealer's default and the collateral's outcome increases, so does the dealer–hedge fund margin. These predictions reconcile the aforementioned evidence of a run on repo: a sharp reduction in repo volumes between dealers and cash lenders, and an increase in repo haircuts between dealers and their prime brokerage clients. The paper also provides new empirical evidence supporting the paper's theoretical results regarding haircut sensitivities.

The model assumes that money market funds are competitive and, given an initial loan request, price the final debt repayment accordingly. The interaction between dealers and hedge funds is modeled as a Nash bargaining game, where the surplus of the asset's payoff and lending terms are split between players. This modeling choice makes it possible to consider different dealer–hedge fund relationships: Hedge funds may only interact with one prime broker, in effect being captured; or they may use multiple dealers to obtain funding. Hedge funds are also assumed to be optimistic in order to generate surplus and induce trade.

The focus of this paper is to study repo as a means to intermediate funds between cash lenders and cash borrowers. But it is important to note that the main function of some repo markets is to intermediate collateral. In effect, some repo contracts are used to borrow assets in order to sell them, similar to securities lending arrangements. Bottazzi et al. (2012) consider an economy where agents use repo to borrow assets in order to sell them, and study the impact on collateral values and lending terms. Duffie et al. (2002) analyze how the presence of search frictions can affect an asset's pricing and lending terms whenever short sellers need to borrow an asset before selling it. Using data from 10-K SEC filings and estimating the amount of securities pledged to dealers through repos, securities lending, and margin loans, Singh (2011) estimates the total amount of collateral circulation in the global financial system. Although the role of rehypothecation for

---

[1]The relevance of these two assumptions are detailed in subsection 2.3.

3

collateral distribution may be sizable, the focus of this paper repo rehypothecation as a means to intermediate funds.

This paper captures key aspects of repo markets in the United States, which can be separated into two distinct markets. The tri-party repo market is the venue where money funds and securities lenders invest large amounts of their cash holdings with broker dealers. These funds help dealers finance their inventories, but an important fraction is distributed to other financial agents (i.e., prime brokerage clients) through the bilateral market.[2] There have been several studies documenting the size and dynamics of the tri-party market, but relatively little is known about the bilateral market. Martin et al. (2014) estimate the total size of the U.S. repo markets to have been on the order of $3 trillion as of May 2012 and $6.1 trillion in July 2008. Although estimates of the relative size of these markets are hard to gauge, Martin et al. (2014) report that in July 2008, the bilateral market was approximately 60% of the total repo market. The sheer size of these markets, and dealers' role as intermediaries of funds, suggest that any difference in contracting terms can have important implications for dealers' access to liquidity. Moreover, these differences can shed light on which counterparty bears the risk in case of a dealer default. Using similar data similar to that in Copeland et al. (2014), this paper reports differences in haircuts from bilateral and tri-party markets and finds considerable differences for some collateral classes.

The above implies that the difference in haircut dynamics reported by Krishnamurthy et al. (2014) and Gorton and Metrick (2012) arises because they study two different markets: tri-party and bilateral repo. Krishnamurthy et al. (2014) recognize that there may be important differences in the dynamics between these two markets, which depend on the relevant frictions counterparties face in each. In particular, they mention that dealers may be altering conditions to their clients in order to improve their cash position: "a rise in interdealer haircuts could indicate a credit crunch in which dealers act defensively given their own capital and liquidity problems, raising credit terms to their borrowers." Copeland et al. (2014) mention that the different margin dynamics between these two markets is somewhat of a puzzle. Martin et al. (2014) argue that margin differences stem from institutional arrangements: tri-party terms are "sticky" (fixed custodial agreements), whereas bilateral terms are negotiated trade by trade. This paper offers an alternative explanation, which stems directly from primary dealers' role as intermediaries between these two markets and the relevant frictions at play.

To support the model's main predictions on haircut sensitivities, this paper uses the same confidential haircut data shown in Copeland et al. (2014) for the U.S. bilateral and tri-party repo markets. Specifically, the model predicts that bilateral margins should respond to changes in co-movements between asset values

---

[2]Adrian et al. (2013) have a good summary on the interactions between these markets. For earlier work on dealers' role as cash intermediaries see Mitchell and Pulvino (2012).

and dealers' default probabilities, while tri-party repo haircuts should only be sensitive to the underlying collateral's characteristics. Preliminary results show that the correlation between collateral values and dealer solvency does have a negative and statistically significant effect on bilateral haircuts. In addition, the evidence shows that tri-party haircuts are relatively insensitive to overall dealer riskiness. Surprisingly, in some specifications the effect of collateral volatility on tri-party haircuts contradicts the natural intuition that higher volatility implies higher haircuts, although these effects are economically small.

This paper is related to the theoretical literature on the use of collateral and its impact on asset prices studied by Geanakoplos (2010), Fostel and Geanakoplos (2011), and Simsek (2013). These models consider a general equilibrium framework, in which differences in agents beliefs can have important effects on what contracts trade in equilibrium. This paper is also related to the work by Brunnermeier and Pedersen (2009), who study margin dynamics whenever financiers (i.e., lenders) use a value-at-risk rule to determine margins. Those papers view collateral markets as a direct means of funding for ultimate investors or arbitrageurs. The focus of this paper is to study the pricing of a specific type of contract (i.e., repo) though the perspective of dealers intermediating funds between borrowers and lenders, and it sheds light on important risks in the current financial environment: a withdrawal from intermediaries' end borrowers.

Duffie (2013) highlights that an important source of vulnerability in the financial system is the potential run of prime brokerage clients from their dealers, which has yet to be addressed in the policy discussion. In effect, a dealer's ability to access their clients' assets is an important resource for the dealer bank's business; not only for financing, but for other activities such as collateral circulation. Duffie (2013) states that the use of client assets to attract funds is an important source of liquidity: "any difference between haircuts (over-collateralization) applied to prime brokerage clients and haircuts applied to prime brokers represents an effective source of additional cash financing to the prime broker." This paper provides the microfoundations for this behavior, endogenizing the haircuts on both sides of the intermediation process and showing that collateral runs are an important source of vulnerability. Eren (2014) also explores the role of dealers as repo intermediaries, arguing that the size of the dealer–cash borrower's haircut depends on the total volume of funds provided by cash lenders and on the dealer's need to replace any liquidity shortfall. In this paper, I consider varying market structures between dealers and hedge funds, and the final equilibrium endogenizes both repo margins which are pinned down by the relevant frictions in the model. Specifically, margins depend on the underlying asset's risk, the relative market power between dealer and hedge fund, the dealer's preference for liquidity and probability of default, and co-movements between collateral values and the dealer's default probability.

The rest of the paper is organize as follows. Section 2 presents the model's environment, its main frictions, and a discusses their relevance. Section 3 presents the formal problem and the main equilibrium results.

Section 4 discusses the model outcome in more detail and relates it to the existing empirical evidence. Section 5 provides some additional evidence of the importance of the intermediation channel and the new empirical evidence supporting the model's prediction on haircut sensitivities. Finally, Section 6 discusses future work and concludes.

2 Model Setup

The model consists of two periods, $t \in \{0, 1\}$. In the first period the initial repo and reverse repo are issued to the dealer and hedge fund respectively, and in the final period the loans are repaid. I assume that the hedge fund cannot bypass the dealer and receive funds directly from money market funds.[3] A detailed discussion of the model's assumptions is provided below.

2.1 Assets & Contracts

There is one risky asset with an uncertain payoff in the second period, $\tilde{a}$. The asset is distributed $G(\cdot)$ under an objective probability distribution with finite support: $[\underline{a}, \overline{a}]$. Under this probability measure, the asset's value in period 1 is $a = \mathbb{E}(\tilde{a})$, which is assumed to be its trading price.

The hedge fund will receive a repo from the dealer to purchase asset $\tilde{a}$ which also serves as collateral on the loan. For the intermediation between the hedge fund and dealer, the initial loan is denoted $a - m^H$ and the final payment in the following period is F^H, making the pair (m^H, F^H) the contracting terms for that repo. Simultaneously, the dealer receives the collateral and posts it with the money fund to raise cash for the loan issued to the hedge fund. The money fund's initial loan is denoted $a - m^M$ and the final debt repayment is F^M. Figure 1 shows the initial leg of the rehypothecation channel, where the dealer receives $(a - m^M)$ from the money market fund and distributes $(a - m^H)$ to the hedge fund, netting $m^H - m^M$. Figure 2 shows the closing leg, where the dealer receives F^H from the hedge fund and distributes F^M to the money market fund, netting $F^H - F^M$.

If the dealer were to default, neither the hedge fund nor the money fund have recourse to the dealer's assets. In contrast the dealer does have access to the hedge fund's assets above and beyond the repo collateral. [4] The model also takes into account the possibility that the dealer's solvency may be correlated with the asset's outcome, which will be detailed in the following subsection.

The money market fund industry is assumed to be competitive and, given the initial loan amount, prices the final debt repayment such that they break even. The outcome between the hedge fund and dealer is

---

[3]This could be due to a severe "lemons" problem money funds face when dealing with hedge funds, or alternatively regulatory restrictions.

[4]See subsection 2.3 for more details.

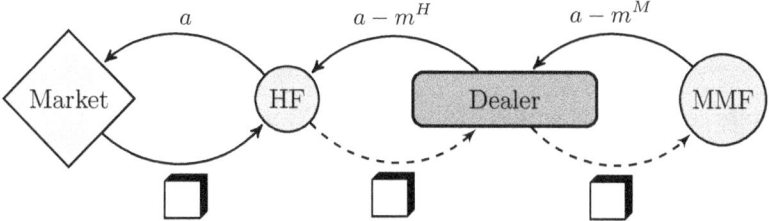

Figure 1: Initial Leg of Rehypothecation with No Default

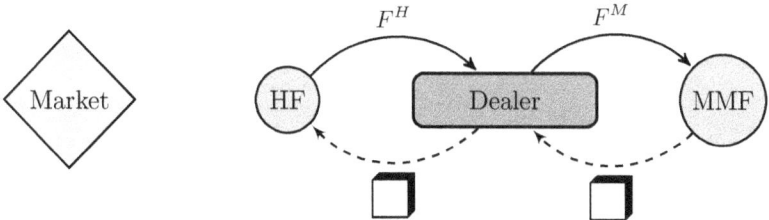

Figure 2: Closing Leg of Rehypothecation with No Default

the result of a Nash bargaining game, wherein the dealer and hedge fund have market power of θ and $1 - \theta$ respectively.

2.2 Agents

The three agents in the model is the original cash lender (the money market fund), the ultimate cash borrower (the hedge fund), and the intermediary between them (the dealer).

2.2.1 Dealer

The dealer's payoff takes the following form:

$$
\begin{aligned}
\mathbb{E}\left(U^D(m^H, F^H, m^M, F^M)\right) &= p\left[\mathbb{E}\left(v(\text{``payoff today''})\right) + \mathbb{E}\left(\text{``payoff tomorrow''}\right)\right] \\
&= p\left[v(m^H - m^M) + \left(F^H + \int_{\underline{a}}^{m^H + F^H - W}(\eta + W - m^H - F^H)dG(\eta) - F^M\right)\right]
\end{aligned}
$$

where $1 - p$ is the dealers' exogenous probability of default and W is the hedge fund's initial endowment. The dealers preference for money in $t = 0$ is modeled by v with $v'(x) > 1$ for $x < a$ and $v'' < 0$. In the initial leg, the dealer nets $m^H - m^M$, getting a payoff of $v(m^H - m^M)$. In $t = 1$ the dealer receives the full repayment F^H if the hedge fund is solvent and, since the dealer has recourse, the repo's collateral and the hedge fund's remaining portfolio if not. The dealer's payoff in $t = 1$ is the risk-neutral valuation of the hedge fund's debt (with recourse) minus the repayment to the money market fund.

The dealer can only default because of exogenous reasons, in which case its payoff is zero. The dealer will face a budget constraint in $t = 0$ and $t = 1$, ensuring the dealer's ability to finance and repay both repos. Therefore, the dealer cannot default because of the intermediation process.[5] Given that the dealer defaults independent of its rehypothecation activity, this also affects its outside option (i.e., not intermediating the repo) which is simply $pv(0) := pv_0$. Therefore, the payoff's dependence on p can be omitted in the intermediation problem.

In addition, the model allows for the dealer's default and the asset's outcome to be correlated. Specifically,

$$\mathbb{P}(\text{dealer solvent}|\tilde{a} = \underline{a}) = \rho,$$

with $\rho \in [0, p]$. If $\rho = p$, then the asset outcome is independent of the asset's outcome. As ρ decreases, the dealers solvency depends on the asset's innovation, to the point where the dealer necessarily defaults whenever $\tilde{a} = \underline{a}$: that is, when $\rho = 0$. Using Bayes' rule, the asset's conditional distribution is denoted by $G(\cdot|s)$ or $G(\cdot|i)$ whenever the dealer is solvent or insolvent, respectively.

2.2.2 Hedge Fund

The hedge fund is an optimistic risk neutral agent, where this optimism generates gains from trade. He is the residual claimant of the repo and internalizes the possibility of a dealer's default. In such a case, the dealer will lose the asset. This entails a loss of the asset's upside relative to the repurchase price: that is, $(\tilde{a} - F^H)^+$. The hedge fund's payoff takes the following form:

$$\hat{\mathbb{E}}\left(U^H(m^H, F^H)\right) = p \int_{m^H + F^H - W}^{\overline{a}} (\eta + W - m^H - F^H) d\hat{G}(\eta) + (1-p) \int_{m^H + F^H - W}^{\overline{a}} (W - m^H + (\eta - F^H)^-) d\hat{G}(\eta),$$

where $\hat{G}$ is the hedge fund's optimistic distribution, with $\hat{\mathbb{E}}(\tilde{a}) = \hat{a} > a$ under the $\hat{G}$ cdf. The hedge fund's outside option is its initial endowment W and the margin m^H must be lower than W in order to finance the asset purchase. Note that in case of a dealer's default, if the hedge fund's repurchase price is higher than the asset value, the hedge fund must pay $(\tilde{a} - F)$. [6]

2.2.3 Money Market Fund

The money market fund gives the initial loan to the dealer, internalizing the dealer's default. Because repo is exempt from automatic stay, the money market fund has immediate access to the collateral, allowing it

---

[5] Even with the aforementioned budget constraints, the dealer may potentially have a shortfall if the hedge fund defaults though this is not a problem in equilibrium, since the promised payment to the money market fund will be the lowest outcome of the asset, ensuring the collateral will always make the money fund whole.

[6] See subsection 2.3 for more details.

to liquidate the collateral in order to make its claim whole.[7] All cash flows above and beyond the face value of the original repo must be returned to the borrower. Therefore, the money fund's net payoff is given by,

$$
\mathbb{E}\left(U^M(m^M, F^M)\right) = pu^M(F^M) + (1-p)\left[u^M(F^M)(1-G(F^M)) + \int_{\underline{a}}^{F^M} u^M(\eta)dG(\eta)\right] - u^M(a-m^M)
$$

with $u^{M'} > 0$ and $u^{M''} < 0$. I assume a competitive money market fund industry, thus in equilibrium they break even.

2.3 Discussion of Assumptions

In this section I briefly discuss the justification and intuition behind the main assumptions driving the equilibrium outcome between counterparties.

Dealer Preferences for Liquidity

In the model, dealers have a preference for holding liquidity in $t = 0$. The dealers' preference for cash in $t = 0$ gives them incentives to have a higher margin when lending to the hedge fund and a lower margin when borrowing from the money fund. This can be motivated in several ways. Dealers may use these funds to finance other areas of their business, effectively using the cash windfall for more profitable activities. It may also reflect a dealer's need for liquidity in times of market stress. In effect, it is precisely when a dealer is perceived to be vulnerable that their need for liquidity is at its highest.

In the base model, changes in the dealer's probability of default do not alter its preference for money in $t = 0$. But in an extension, discussed in Section 4, incorporating this feature can explain an increase in margin in the bilateral market, while maintaining the lending terms constant in the tri-party market. This reconciles different views on the dynamics of these markets during the 2007–09 crisis.

Recourse vs. Non-Recourse

In the model it is assumed that neither the hedge fund nor the money fund have access to a dealer's balance sheet in case of default. In theory, if either counterparty suffers a loss in their contract, they have an unsecured claim on the bankrupt dealer since repos are recourse loans. Although these firms are entitled to receive additional payments if they are not made whole, in reality the costly and tedious task of resolving a large broker dealer may significantly hinder this process. For example, given the contracting nature between money funds and their own clients, awaiting the resolution of a bankruptcy process may trigger a run on the money fund itself. Since in the U.S. repos are exempt from automatic stay, which gives the money fund the ability to liquidate the collateral immediately, money funds would have a strong

---

[7]Automatic stay is a U.S. bankruptcy provision that prohibits creditors from collecting payments from a borrower who files for bankruptcy. Under current U.S. law, repos are exempt from automatic stay, allowing lenders to immediately sell the collateral in case of default.

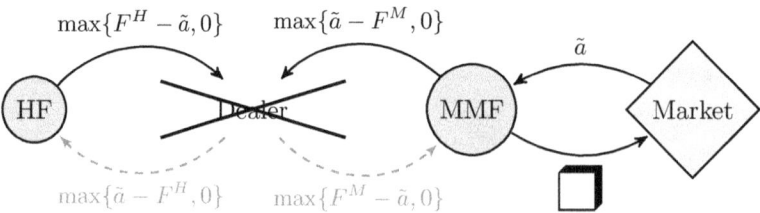

Figure 3: Cash Flows Upon Dealer Default

incentive to completely insulate themselves from the dealer. Thus, even if the dealer had some remaining assets to distribute in bankruptcy, the money market fund would still desire to make the repo risk-free. In the model, this translates into having to heavily compensate the money fund for being exposed to a dealer's default, in which case the money fund receives nothing but the asset itself.

The non-recourse assumption of the hedge fund to the dealer also has important consequences. In the model, the bankruptcy resolution between the dealer and hedge fund is asymmetric. In effect, if the dealer defaults, the hedge fund loses the upside on the collateral relative to the repurchase price. But if the asset's value is below the contracted loan repayment, the hedge fund must pay the shortfall to the bankruptcy estate. Ex ante, this cost is proportional to the hedge fund's initial margin. The hedge fund's loss when the dealer defaults can be justified by the same arguments mentioned above: It may be very costly for the hedge fund to wait for the resolution of a lengthy bankruptcy process to receive payments on any unsecured claim. Although this might be a strong assumption for a hedge fund, which presumably may be more patient than a money market fund, the considerable costs associated with the default of a large prime broker would make the recovery of unsecured claims more unlikely. In addition, the hedge fund's obligation to pay an asset shortfall relative to the repurchase price can be interpreted as the dealer's ability to seize their clients portfolio in case of any outstanding balance, irrespective of their bankruptcy status.[8] Thus, it is reasonable to assume that conditional on the dealers default, the hedge fund would not expect any unsecured claims on the dealer to be fulfilled (at least not immediately), but would expect to pay any outstanding balances it could have.

Figure 3 highlights the relevant cash flows after a dealers default. The money market fund sells the asset to the market, and both the hedge fund and the money fund owe the dealer any positive balance that may be owed (black lines). The asymmetric non-recourse assumption implies that any obligation owed by the dealer will not be fulfilled (dashed red lines).

The consequences of the recourse assumption is that both of the dealer's counterparties stand to take a loss in case of default. This implies that the money market fund will want to insulate itself from the dealer,

---

[8]I'd like to thank Mark Carlson for noting the dealer's ability to easily seize clients assets if there are any outstanding balances due. Eren (2014) also assumes this type of bankruptcy asymmetry between dealers and cash borrowers.

and that the hedge fund and dealer have to balance this cost with the dealer's preference for liquidity. Once the equilibrium is characterized, Section 4 will revisit these issues in light of the final outcome.

3   Intermediation Problem & Equilibrium

This section formalizes the intermediation problem and presents the resulting equilibrium. Given the above setting, dealers and hedge funds enter a Nash bargaining problem, setting the terms of both the dealer's repo and reverse repo to split the surplus between them. The problem can be summarized as

$$\max_{\{m^H, m^M, F^H, F^M\}} \left(\mathbb{E}\left(U^D(m^H, F^H, m^M, F^M) \right) - v_0 \right)^\theta \left(\mathbb{E}\left(U^H(m^H, F^H) \right) - W \right)^{1-\theta}$$

subject to

$$m^H \geq m^M \qquad\qquad \text{Initial Leg Self Financing}$$

$$m^H + F^H \geq m^M + F^M \quad \text{Overall Financing}$$

$$\mathbb{E}\left(U^M(m^M, F^M) \right) = 0 \quad \text{MMF Break Even}$$

$$m^H \leq W \qquad\qquad \text{HF Down Payment Constraint}$$

$$m^H, m^M, F^H, F^M \geq 0.$$

The problem's objective function is the Nash bargaining game between the dealer and hedge fund. The first restriction ensures that the initial loan from the money market fund is enough to finance the hedge fund's repo. The second restriction ensures that the overall financing conditions are met. The third restriction is the money market funds break even condition. The fourth restriction ensures that the hedge fund has a large enough endowment to pay the initial loans margin to purchase the asset. The final restrictions are so that the contracting terms are feasible.

To simplify the analysis, I will restrict the study to analyze a binomial risky asset. Under the objective probability distribution, the asset pays $\bar{a}$ with probability α and $\underline{a}$ with probability $1 - \alpha$. The hedge fund's optimism is manifested through a higher probability of a good outcome: $\hat{\alpha} > \alpha$. The following theorem characterizes an equilibrium of this model.[9] The proof is relegated to the appendix.

Theorem 1 (Solution to Intermediary Problem). *In the intermediary problem with a binomial asset payoff, if the following parameter assumptions hold:*

i) $\frac{\hat{\alpha}}{p} \left\{ \frac{p - \rho(1-\alpha)}{p - \rho(1-\hat{\alpha})} \right\} + \frac{\rho}{p}(1 - \alpha) < \frac{1}{1 - (1-\alpha)(1-\rho)}$

ii) $p(\hat{a} - \underline{a}) \geq W$

---

[9]To simplify this version of the model I only present one possible equilibrium. More equilibria may be characterized with similar properties.

iii) $m^* := (v')^{-1}\left(\frac{\hat{a}}{p}\left\{\frac{p-\rho(1-\alpha)}{p-\rho(1-\hat{\alpha})}\right\} + \frac{\rho}{p}(1-\alpha)\right) + (a - \underline{a}) \leq W$

with $\rho \in [0, p]$, then there exits a θ^S and $\underline{\theta}$ such that:

for $\theta \in [\theta^S, 1)$ an equilibrium $(m^{H*}, F^{H*}, m^{M*}, F^{F*})$ is given by $F^{H*} = \theta F_{MonoD} + (1-\theta)F_{MonoH}$ where,

$$F_{MonoD} = \bar{a} - \frac{((1-\hat{\alpha})W + \hat{\alpha}m^H)}{p - \rho(1 - \hat{\alpha})}$$

$$F_{MonoH} = \underline{a} - \frac{v(m^* - (a - \underline{a})) - v_0 + \frac{\rho(1-\alpha)}{p}(W - m^*)}{\left(1 - \frac{\rho(1-\alpha)}{p}\right)}$$

and $m^{H*} = m^*, F^{H*} = F^*, m^{M*} = a - \underline{a}, F^{M*} = \underline{a}$, and

for $\theta \in (\underline{\theta}, \theta^S]$ an equilibrium $(m^{H*}, F^{H*}, m^{M*}, F^{F*})$ is given by the solution to

$$m^{H*} + F^{H*} = W + \underline{a} \quad and \quad \frac{(1-\theta)\left(\mathbb{E}\left(U^D\right) - v_0\right)}{\theta(\hat{\mathbb{E}}\left(U^H\right) - W)} = \frac{v'(m^{H*} - m^{M*}) - 1}{(1-p) - (1-\hat{\alpha})(1-\rho)}$$

with $m^{M*} = a - \underline{a}, F^{M*} = \underline{a}$.

Proof. See Appendix □

The theorem focuses on equilibria that can separate both the dealer–hedge fund problem and the dealer–money market fund problem, i.e., the financing conditions are slack. This is to focus the discussion on the frictions present in each of the intermediaries interactions, without considering the dealers hard financing constraints. The solution is divided into two sub intervals, which imply risky or safe contracting terms for the hedge fund.

The dealer–money fund is relatively straight forward for the entire feasible range: charge the highest margin that results in a risk-free contract for the money fund. Since the agents' relationship does not have recourse, any increase in repurchase price above the lowest asset outcome will entail a potential loss, for which the money market fund must be compensated. Although the dealer has a preference for money today (since $v'(\cdot) > 1$), increasing the money funds initial loan, this preference implies a disproportionately high repurchase price. In effect, comparing the two agents' marginal rate of substitution between (m^M, F^M) in the proposed equilibrium gives

$$v'(m^* - (a - \underline{a})) < \frac{1}{1 - (1-\alpha)(1-\rho)}, \tag{1}$$

where the Left Hand Side (LHS) is the marginal utility increase in lowering m^M and the Right Hand Side (RHS) is the additional dollar needed to compensate the money market fund.

The range of feasible θ is given by the interval $(\underline{\theta}, 1)$, which is divided into two by θ^S. For relatively high values of θ the dealer–hedge fund problem results in risky contract for the hedge fund. In this case, equalizing the agents' marginal rate of substitution, the condition that pins down m^{H*} is given by the solution to the following equation,[10]

$$\frac{v'(m^H - m^M) - \frac{\rho(1-\alpha)}{p}}{1 - \frac{\rho(1-\alpha)}{p}} = \frac{\hat{\alpha}}{p\left(1 - \frac{\rho(1-\hat{\alpha})}{p}\right)} \tag{2}$$

Equation (2) highlights the two main frictions at play. The (LHS) is the dealer's marginal rate of substitution: Increasing m^H increases the amount of cash in the initial leg valued at v, but it lowers the recovery if the hedge fund defaults whenever the dealer is solvent (with probability $\frac{\rho(1-\alpha)}{p}$); meanwhile, an increase in F^H increases the dealer's payoff if the hedge fund avoids default (with probability $1 - \frac{\rho(1-\alpha)}{p}$). The (RHS) is the hedge funds marginal rate of substitution: Increasing m^H lowers its initial endowment stock which lowers its payoff if the hedge fund avoids default, irrespective of the dealer's solvency (with probability $\hat{\alpha}$); however, increasing F^H only affects its payoff if the dealer does not default and the asset has a good outcome (with probability $p\left(1 - \frac{\rho(1-\hat{\alpha})}{p}\right)$), since any asset upside is forfeited otherwise.

The dealer–hedge fund's final repurchase price is a convex combination of their respective repurchase price if each were a monopolist: F_{MonoD} and F_{MonoH}, respectively. In effect, condition (ii) ensures that the dealer's monopolist solution results in a risky repo for the hedge fund (i.e., the hedge fund may default); therefore, a high value of θ will give the aforementioned solution, which decreases as the dealers market power is diminished. The cutoff θ^S occurs when the optimal dealer–hedge fund contract is risk free. Note that conditions (2) and (1) hold simultaneously due to assumptions (i) and (iii).

For $\theta \in (\underline{\theta}, \theta^S]$ the dealer hedge fund contract is risk-free, so the dealer forfeits margin to the hedge fund, but total debt burden $(m^{H*} + F^{H*})$ remains constant. As the hedge fund's bargaining position becomes stronger, either the loss in margin is so severe that equation (1) is violated or $m^{H*} + F^{H*} < \underline{a} + W$, which pins down $\underline{\theta}$. In effect, in the first case the loss of liquidity from the hedge fund's contract creates incentives for the dealer to increase m^{M*}, implying a risky contract for the money fund. The definition of $\underline{\theta}$ focuses on equilibria where the money fund's contract is risk-free and the overall debt burden is greater or equal to $W + \underline{a}$.[11]

Note that the optimal solution is in fact self-financing since $m^{H*} > m^{M*}$ and $m^{H*} + F^{H*} \geq \underline{a} + W > \underline{a}$. Therefore, the dealer does reap benefits from the difference in margin, gaining liquidity today without having to suffer any financing costs; and even if the hedge fund defaults, the dealer is able to repay the money fund. In other words the dealer receives a liquidity windfall.

---

[10]Which is feasible given assumption iii).

[11]This assumption just serves to limit the amount of equilibrium considered and is not absolutely necessary for the main result.

3.1 Equilibrium when Default and Asset Outcome are Independent ($\rho = p$)

The main results of the paper can be appreciated in a simplified case, when $\tilde{a}$ is independent from the dealer's survival. Having characterized the repo intermediation equilibrium it is important to understand how the feasibility of such an equilibrium can change with p. The following proposition shows how the bargaining power threshold is altered for different levels of dealer solvency.

Proposition 1 (Feasibility as Dealer Risk Changes). *Given the equilibrium characterized in Theorem 1 with $\rho = p$ and p sufficiently close to 1, then the lower bound threshold $\underline{\theta}$ is decreasing in p.*

Proof. See Appendix □

Proposition 1 shows that the interval in which the equilibrium involves a riskless contract for the money market fund and a feasible outcome for the hedge fund and dealer shrinks as the dealer's probability of default increases. Thus, it is harder for less solvent dealers to engage in repo intermediation, precisely because the collateral provider has reduced incentives to participate.

Another important issue is to understand how the terms of trade change for different levels of dealer counterparty risk. The first result shows how the margin changes under the original specification.

Proposition 2 (Margins as Dealer Risk Changes). *Given the equilibrium characterized in Theorem 1 with $\rho = p$, for $\theta \in [\theta^S, 1)$,*

$$\frac{\partial m^{H*}}{\partial p} = -\frac{\alpha}{p^2 v''(m^{H*} - (a - \underline{a}))} > 0,$$

and for $\theta \in (\underline{\theta}, \theta^S]$,

$$\frac{\partial m^{H*}}{\partial p} = \frac{\theta(v'(m^* - (a - \underline{a})) - 1)\hat{\alpha}(\bar{a} - F^{*H}) + (1 - \theta)\left(\mathbb{E}\left(U^D\right) - v_0\right)}{\hat{\alpha}(1 - p)(v'(m^* - (a - \underline{a})) - 1) - v''(m^{H*} - (a - \underline{a}))\theta(\mathbb{E}\left(U^H\right) - W)} > 0.$$

Proof. Both results are derived directly from taking the implicit derivative of the first-order condition that pins down m^{H*}. For $\theta \in [\theta^S, 1)$ this is equation (2) and for $\theta \in (\underline{\theta}, \theta^S]$ this is equation $\frac{(1-\theta)\left(\mathbb{E}(U^D) - v_0\right)}{\theta(\mathbb{E}(U^H) - W)} = \frac{v'(m^{H*} - m^{M*}) - 1}{\hat{\alpha}(1 - p)}$. □

The result in Proposition 2 indicates that as the dealer's probability of remaining solvent increases so does the dealer–hedge fund margin. Although this result is rather unsatisfactory, it is very intuitive. In effect, as the dealers probability of default decreases (i.e., as p increases), the hedge funds unsecured claims are less important, which increases the surplus in the relationship maximized via equation (2). That is, the tradeoff between the hedge fund's loss and the dealer's preference for liquidity is changed because the loss is smaller. Therefore, a larger margin is optimal.

14

But the result in Proposition 2 can be easily overturned by considering a slight modification to the model: specifically if one assumes that the dealer's marginal preference for cash today decreases with its solvency. That is, if $\frac{\partial v'(\cdot)}{\partial p}$ is sufficiently negative; the optimal response is an increase in margin whenever the dealer is closer to default.[12] This additional condition can be easily understood by considering that the dealer's liquidity needs increase as its probability of default increases.

Proposition 3 (**Margins as Dealer Risk Changes — Alternate Model**). *Given the equilibrium characterized in Theorem 1 with $\rho = p$ and assuming that $\frac{\partial v'(\cdot)}{\partial p} < -\frac{\alpha}{p^2}$, then for $\theta \in [\theta^S, 1)$,*

$$\frac{\partial m^{H*}}{\partial p} = -\frac{1}{v''(m^{H*} - (a - \underline{a}))} \left(\frac{\partial v'(m^{H*} - (a - \underline{a}))}{\partial p} + \frac{\alpha}{p^2} \right) < 0.$$

Proof. The result is derived directly by taking the implicit derivative of the first order condition that pins down m^{H*} — i.e., equation (2). $\square$

Proposition 3 states that if the dealers preference for liquidity decreases with its solvency, then the optimal contract will prescribe an increase in the margin offered to the hedge fund, even though it is costly.[13] The reduced surplus from increasing the hedge fund's cost in case of a dealer's default is outweighed by the dealer's need for liquidity in times of market stress.

3.2 Equilibrium when Default and Asset Outcome are Correlated ($\rho < p$)

In this subsection I analyze how the contracting terms change whenever the dealer's default is correlated with the repo's collateral, particularly how the dealer–hedge fund margin changes as ρ decreases.

Proposition 4 (**Margins as Correlation Changes**). *Given the equilibrium characterized in Theorem 1 with $\rho < 1$ and assuming that $\frac{1-\alpha}{p} - \frac{\hat{\alpha}-\alpha}{(p-\rho(1-\hat{\alpha}))^2} > 0$, then for $\theta \in [\theta^S, 1)$,*

$$\frac{\partial m^{H*}}{\partial \rho} = \frac{1}{v''(m^{H*} - (a - \underline{a}))} \left\{ \frac{1-\alpha}{p} - \frac{\hat{\alpha}-\alpha}{(p-\rho(1-\hat{\alpha}))^2} \right\} < 0.$$

Proof. The result is derived directly by taking the implicit derivative of the first order condition that pins down m^{H*}, i.e., equation (2). $\square$

Proposition 4 shows the conditions under which an increase in the correlation implies a higher dealer–hedge fund margin. The intuition behind the result stems from the fact that the hedge fund's loss of the asset in case of a dealer default only has a negative impact if the asset has a good outcome. In effect, when

---

[12]An example of this characteristic with power utility is: $v(x) = a^{\eta/p} \left(\frac{x^{1-\eta/p}}{1-\eta/p} \right)$.

[13]A similar condition can be derived for $\theta \in (\underline{\theta}, \theta^S]$.

the dealer defaults, the hedge fund's payoff stemming from the asset is $(\tilde{a} - F^H)^-$. Therefore, if it is more likely for the dealer to default whenever the asset outcome is bad, then the expected hedge fund loss is smaller implying a higher dealer–hedge fund margin.

3.3 Numerical Example

Figure 4 illustrates the properties of the equilibrium characterized in Theorem 1 when $\rho = p$ for a given parameterization. The dealer's preference for cash in $t = 0$ is modeled as power utility with $\eta < 1$, that is,

$$v(x) = a^\eta \left(\frac{x^{1-\eta}}{1-\eta} \right).$$

Given that the dealer–money fund contract is constant, the focus is on the dealer–hedge fund outcome. For θ close to 1, the solution approaches the dealer-monopolist contract, where the overall lending terms $m^{H*} + F^{H*}$ are at their highest. As the dealer's market power decreases the overall lending terms decrease, but the margin is held constant, satisfying equation (2) which maximizes the surplus between borrower and lender. In effect, the condition in equation (2) balances the cost of the hedge fund's loss in case of default with the dealer's preference for cash upfront.

A constant margin implies a reduction in the repurchase price until $\theta = \theta^S$, when the equilibrium switches to a riskless contract between the dealer and the hedge fund. In this case, the balance of power leads to a more favorable margin for the hedge fund at the cost of a higher repurchase price, while the overall debt burden remains constant. Here, the hedge fund is able to reduce its unsecured claim, costing the dealer the marginal benefit of more cash initially.

Figure 5 shows the resulting equilibrium in terms of the usual repo contracting terms — i.e., haircut and repo rate. The mapping of the initial margin and final repurchase price to the repo haircut and repo rate is given by

$$\text{haircut} = 1 - \frac{a - m^{H*}}{a} \quad \& \quad \text{repo rate} = \frac{F^{H*}}{a - m^{H*}} - 1.$$

Note that the intuition of the model remains: As the hedge fund's bargaining position increases, the haircut and the corresponding repo rate decrease.

4 Model Discussion

Theorem 1 sheds light on a number of important features of the model that are relevant for the repo intermediation process. First, note that while the risk-free dealer–money fund repo is a feature often assumed in the literature, it arises endogenously in this model.[14] In effect, since the money fund must be heavily compensated for the dealer's default, the optimal agreement insulates the money fund from the dealer altogether, leaving only the collateral.[15] In the model, this occurs because the money fund has no recourse to the dealer's other assets in case of default. Given the lengthy, and presumably costly, resolution of a large financial firm and the immediate liquidity that money market funds must provide to their clients, it is reasonable that the money fund would want to insulate itself from the dealer's counterparty risk. Moreover, this result is in line with the common perception that repos in the tri-party market are relatively safe investment vehicles.

The second interesting feature is that whenever $\rho = p$, as p decreases this class of equilibrium is harder to sustain, which is the result of Proposition 1. This is simply observed in the setup of the problem: When the dealers probability of default increases, the importance of the hedge fund's "dead weight loss" through its unsecured claim also increases. Note that there would still be a cost to the hedge fund even if the strong norecourse assumption were relaxed. In effect, if the hedge fund had access to any cashflows of the asset sale above and beyond the money market fund's repurchase price, the hedge fund would suffer an ex ante loss proportional to $m^{H*} - m^{M*}$ instead of m^{H*}. That is, the frictionless unsecured claim of the hedge fund is the additional cash that the dealer reaps through intermediation. Although this version of the model complicates the analysis, the message is the same: The hedge fund holds an unsecured claim on the dealer and thus has incentives to run. Therefore, an increased probability of a dealer default decreases the likelihood of the intermediation of repos, which is induced by a run from collateral providers rather than cash lenders who (endogenously) are not subject to the dealer's counterparty risk.

Together, these two points put together capture the empirical findings of Krishnamurthy et al. (2014), and (partly) Copeland et al. (2014), who show that, conditional on the underlying collateral's asset class, there is a high degree of homogeneity in haircuts among dealers in the tri-party repo market: that is, the margin is largely asset-specific. Krishnamurthy et al. (2014) go on to document relatively stable haircuts the tri-party market and a sharp contraction in the amount of repos issued with riskier collateral classes, such as non-Agency MBS/ABS. This can be interpreted as a run from collateral providers, which eliminates the intermediation process altogether. In the model, margins in the tri-party market only depend on the riskiness of the collateral, thus tri-party repo haircuts are allowed to increase, but this increase is only asset-specific. The near-constant margin in the U.S. Treasury market documented by Krishnamurthy et al. (2014) is in line with this model outcome.

In addition, Theorem 1 can account for an increase in margin in the bilateral market, leaving the tri-

---

[14]This result is also arises endogenously in Infante (2013) due to the borrower's ability to dilute existing creditors.

[15]Note that a similar version of this result would also arise under more general asset payoff distributions if one considers the money fund to be relatively more risk averse.

party margin unchanged. Perhaps the most surprising result is how changes in the joint distribution of asset outcome and dealer solvency affect bilateral contracting terms. In effect, Proposition 4 shows that an increase in the correlation between the dealer's solvency and the asset outcome actually increases the margin in the dealer–hedge fund relationship. Intuitively, the hedge funds loss is largest when the dealer defaults after having rehypothecated a highly valued asset. Thus, if this state of the world is more likely, the optimal hedge fund haircut should be lower.

The consequences of changes in dealer default risk are mixed. In Proposition 2, as the dealer's probability of default increases, the expected margin loss to the hedge fund also increases, resulting in the optimal contract prescribing a lower bilateral haircut. But incorporating the assumption that an increase in default probability heightens a dealer's preference for cash overturns the result. In effect, Proposition 3 prescribes a bilateral margin increase whenever the dealer's probability of default increases by introducing a relationship between the dealer's marginal preference for a dollar today and its probability of default. For example, if a primary dealer were to be in distress due to low asset valuations stemming from a fire sale, or because alternative financing lines were reduced, then the dealer would have a stronger desire to obtain cash from other activities.

These results can be reconciled with Gorton and Metrick (2012)'s findings of a sharp increase in haircuts during the financial crisis. The argument of this paper is that either the correlation between dealer's portfolio and their solvency increased, or the dealer's need for liquidity increased. The effect of both of these channels is that dealers captured more funds in the initial intermediation leg. This is also in line with the survey evidence presented in Copeland et al. (2014), who show a large spread between tri-party and bilateral repo haircuts.

5   Empirical Analysis

This section shows evidence of the importance of this channel by showing data on the total volume in the U.S. repo market and estimating the potential cash windfall that would ensue because of different contracting terms. I also outline an empirical strategy to test the dynamics for bilateral and tri-party margins suggested by the model.

5.1   Estimate of Cash Windfall in Initial Repo Leg

To provide additional evidence of the importance of repo intermediation, I use primary dealers' financing reports collected by the Federal Reserve Bank of New York (FRBNY): FR 2004 C. This survey collects weekly reports on primary dealers' outstanding financing, particularly on the amount of repos and reverse repos. FRBNY releases the dealers' aggregate positions which document the amount of funds received by dealers through repos and the amount of funds issued by dealers through reverse repos.

Between July 2001 and March 2013, repo and reverse repo transactions were reported by aggregating all underlying collateral classes. As prescribed by the model, this omits any contracting differences that may arise from different collateral riskiness. To alleviate this concern, I also show the newly revised survey that starts from April 2013 onwards, where different collateral classes are reported separately.

Given that only the initial loan amounts are reported, the ability of this data to shed light on the amount of liquidity reaped by primary dealers though intermediation is limited. But coupled with existing literature showing the difference in haircuts between tri-party and bilateral repo, the importance of this channel can be gauged. Observing the time series of the minimum between repos and reverse repos, the size of their intermediation (i.e., primary dealers' *matched book*) can be estimated. Though many of these repos are between dealers in the tri-party market[16], evidence reported by Copeland et al. (2012) on the size of the bilateral market suggests that it makes up a sizable fraction of dealers' matched book. In all of the figures presented here, the reverse repo amount is always lower than the repo amount, implying that more money is being lent to the dealers than what is being distributed. In Figures 6 and 7, these time series are labeled "Reverse Repo". Moreover, the difference between repos and reverse repos captures the amount of cash that stays in the dealer sector through their repo operations, which in Figures 6 and 7 is marked as "Net repo borrowing". Note that taking the difference cancels out intra-dealer repos. Although it is unclear what fraction of this difference is due to different contracting schemes (i.e., $m^{H*} - m^{M*}$) and how much can be attributed to dealers funding their position, it does capture the important inflow of cash reaped through the repo market.

Information can be drawn from available estimates of haircuts and their differences to estimate the windfall of cash discussed in this paper — i.e., $m^{H*} - m^{M*}$ (see Figure 8). As noted in Subsection 3.3, gross haircuts are reported as the ratio between the margin and the collateral value. For example, a haircut of ϕ percent corresponds to: $\phi = m/a$. The FR 2004 data provides us with estimates of total inflows — i.e., $loan = a - m$.[17]. Therefore, a rough estimate of the windfall due to intermediation is $(\phi_H - \phi_M) * loan_H$ — that is, the difference in haircuts times the amount of reverse repos.[18] Figure 8 shows that some of these differences were in the order of 5% to 40%, especially at the beginning of the sample, potentially implying large inflows.

Figure 6 shows the aggregate series between July 2001 and March 2013. The measure of the matched

---

[16]Specifically, in the GCF Repo market: see Fleming and Garbade (2003) for details on this interdealer market.

[17]For now I will assume a unique haircut within collateral classes. There is an issue when adding inflows and backing out the total margin in the presence of different haircuts.

[18]This is an upper bound, since the reverse repo number includes interdealer trades.

book shows a sizable intermediation role, on the order of $2 trillion at the end of the sample, and a net cash inflow on the order of $500 billion. Figure 7 shows the more recent information separated by collateral class. For example, the size of the matched book for Agency MBS is between $500 and $300 billion. This implies that a hair cut difference of 5% implies a windfall of $25 to $18 billion, which is about 1/8 of the total cash imputed by the net repo borrowing series. Note that the existing literature documents that the differences in margin are larger in times of market stress, implying a larger reliance on prime brokerage client's assets. This evidence is suggestive to the important channel that repo intermediation can provide for dealers.

5.2 Empirical Strategy to Test Haircut Levels

The model has the following empirical predictions for level of bilateral and tri-party repo haircuts in the rehypothecation chain:

P1) *Bilateral margins are negatively related to an increase in the probability of a dealer's solvency conditional on a bad asset outcome.*

P2) *Tri-party margins are positively related to the underlying collateral's risk and should not depend on dealer characteristics.*

Prediction P2 is a direct consequence of Theorem 1. In effect, a mean-preserving increase in the difference between $\bar{a}$ and $\underline{a}$ (i.e., an increase in volatility) increases the tri-party haircut. Although the current version of the model does not have a direct implication of the impact of collateral volatility on bilateral haircuts, it is reasonable to expect that bilateral haircuts would also increase with asset volatility. Finally, prediction P1 stems from Proposition 4. Recall that the model is not conclusive on the direct relationship between a dealer's default probability and the level of bilateral margins. The above summary motivates the following linear specification:

$$hc_t^i = \beta_0^i + \beta_1^i \sigma_t^{AC} + \beta_2^i DD_t + \beta_3^i \rho_t^{AC,DD} + \gamma^i X_t + \epsilon_t^i \tag{3}$$

where hc_t^i denotes the haircut of either the bilateral market (BI), the tri-party (TPR) market, or the difference between the two (DF); that is, $i \in \{BI, TPR, DF\}$. The collateral's overall riskiness is captured by σ_t^{AC} which represents the underlying collateral's return volatility. The primary dealer's solvency, denoted by DD_t, is captured by the simple average of primary dealers' CDS. The correlation between the level of the underlying asset class and the primary dealer's default probability $\rho_t^{AC,DD}$, captures changes in the model's conditional probability. In effect, if the level of dealers' CDS goes down as asset valuations deteriorate (i.e., if $\rho_t^{AC,DD}$ increases), then all things being equal, the probability of solvency conditional on a bad asset outcome increases.[19] Finally, the controls, X_t, incorporate measures of the repo risk-free rate and overall market volatilities. Therefore, the specification in equation (3) implies that prediction P1 leads to $\beta_3^{BI} < 0$ and prediction P2 leads to $\beta_1^{TPR} > 0$. It is also reasonable to expect that collateral volatility has a positive effect on bilateral haircuts, implying $\beta_1^{BI} > 0$. Although there are no explicit predictions on what happens to the difference in haircuts, the model implies that their sensitivities should be similar to those of bilateral haircuts.

5.2.1 Data

The hardest data to obtain for this empirical analysis are measures of bilateral and tri-party repo haircuts. FRBNY collects confidential data on the U.S. tri-party repo market directly from the clearing banks. This data allows me to compute tri-party repo haircuts for different collateral classes. In addition, FRBNY collects data on bilateral repo haircuts through primary dealer surveys. Although this data merely captures a median of survey responses, it is informative of overall market trends. The data is on a weekly frequency and spans from January 2009 to September 2014.[20] Specific details on these data can be found in Copeland et al. (2014). Given the potentially high degree of measurement error in the bilateral series, I focus the analysis on relatively riskier asset classes. Thus, following the calcification proposed by Copeland et al. (2014), I consider Corporate Debt, Private Label CMO, and Asset-Backed Securities. Figure 8 plots the difference between the bilateral and tri-party haircut for different collateral classes.

Asset class volatility, σ_t^{AC}, is calculated using the 60-day return volatility of indices that track each collateral class. Specifically, for Corporate Debt I use Bank of America Merrill Lynch AAA-A US Corporate Index, and for both Private Label CMO and Asset-Backed Securities I use the ABX BBB Index.[21] The dealer's default probability, DD_t, is calculated using an equally weighted index of Primary Dealer CDS. Finally, $\rho_t^{AC,DD}$ is measured using the 60-day correlation between the asset class index level and the level of DD_t. The control variables are the GCF Treasury repo rate to proxy the repo risk-free rate, and the VIX index or the 60 day volatility of the S&P 500 Index to proxy for overall market riskiness.

All the explanatory variables are demeaned and standardized by their sample average and standard deviation. Note that by only standardizing the explanatory variables, and not the dependent variables, the interpretation of the point estimates are simple: a one standard deviation change in the explanatory variable results in a point estimate change in the haircuts.

---

[19] Of course, changes in $\rho_t^{AC,DD}$ may capture changes in the underlying collateral or primary dealer solvency, but presumably these effects would be captured by σ_t^{AC} and DD_t.

[20] Regrettably, FRBNY changed the survey in September and the match between the new and old surveys is a delicate matter and thus part of future work.

[21] Although the ABX index is perhaps more appropriate to measure changes in the Private Label CMO market, following existing empirical literature, this index is also used to track the subprime mortgage market.

5.3 Empirical Results & Discussion

The preliminary results from regression (3) are found in Table 1, 2, and 3. I show point estimates and t-statistics correcting for autocorrelation using Newey-West. Given the natural autocorrelation from using a 60-day rolling window for volatility and correlation estimates, I report Newey-West t-statistics with an 8 week lag.

Table 1 shows the robust and statistically significant effect of the correlation between dealers' default risk and the underlying asset on bilateral margins. In effect, in almost all of the specifications, β_3^{BI} is statistically negative. The effect is also economically important. For example, looking at results for ABS with no controls, a one standard deviation increase in correlation corresponds to a 2.17% decrease in haircuts. This evidence gives credence to prediction P1.

Table 1 also shows the importance of overall asset riskiness. A positive and statistically significant estimate of β_1^{BI} implies that higher collateral volatility leads to higher bilateral haircuts. Note that in the Corporate Debt specification, the index's volatility is driven out of the regression when measures of overall market volatility are included. Although this is a slight deviation from the original intuition, the message is the same: Higher asset volatility implies higher bilateral haircuts. In addition, note that Table 1 shows no clear effect from the primary dealer's solvency, which is implied by the two contradicting results: Propositoin 2 and Proposition 3.

The results in Table 2 are harder to reconcile with the model. The model's prediction is that the underlying collateral's riskiness positively affects tri-party haircuts and that haircuts are only asset-dependent. The resulting estimates show only a mild effect for ABS collateral, an insignificant effect for Private Label CMO, and a negative effect for Corporate Debt. Even controls for overall market volatility show a negative relationship when significant. These results are counterintuitive, although note that whenever it is significant, the impact on the overall level of margins is relatively small. In effect, the intercept on these regressions indicates that the overall level of haircuts is between 5% and 6%. The overall impact of these counterintuitive results is, at most, approximately 30bps. Therefore, even though the impact is not negligible, economically it is quite small. It is also puzzling to see the VIX and S&P return volatility have a negative effect on Private Label CMO and ABS collateral repo haircuts, which is not captured by the asset volatility estimate. Using a more detailed analysis at the dealer level, similar to Copeland et al. (2014), may shed more light on these dynamics in the tri-party market.

Regression (3) on the difference between bilateral and tri-party haircuts reinforces the main message of the paper. In effect, Table 3 robustly shows that the difference in margin increases with asset volatility. That is, more volatile collateral increases the haircut spread. In addition, the relation between the haircut spread and the correlation between dealer default and asset value is in line with prediction P1. Specifically, the majority of the specifications give a statistically negative relationship, showing that a correlation increase affects the bilateral haircut and consequently reduces the spread between bilateral and tri-party haircuts.

6 Concluding Remarks & Future Work

This paper analyses repo markets as a cash intermediation chain. Dealers receive funds from money market funds through the tri-party market and distribute them to their prime brokerage clients in the bilateral market. This paper shows that different contracting terms in these markets can provide dealers with an important liquidity channel. Moreover, the contracting terms derived from the model imply that collateral providers have more incentives to run than cash lenders, in line with some of the risks highlighted by Duffie (2013). The model also predicts that conditional on the repo collateral class, margins are homogeneous and relatively stable in the tri-party market. In addition, the model predicts that as the correlation between the dealer's default and collateral values increase, the bilateral market haircut will decrease because the probability of losing a valuable asset is greater.

The paper links the results to the existing literature on repo, corroborating some of the stylized facts of these markets in the U.S. during the recent financial crisis. In addition, a preliminary empirical analysis validates the important haircut sensitivities proposed in the model.

One open question that remains is why does the intermediation chain exist in the first place? That is, why don't cash lenders directly fund cash borrowers? Although it is beyond the scope of this paper, one reason may be the relatively opaque nature of cash borrowers. In effect, an important feature of the hedge fund industry is that their positions are largely unknown to outsiders. Thus, cash lenders such as money market funds, would be concerned about the borrower's counterparty risk. Arguably, prime brokers do not suffer such a severe informational problem, since they execute many of the hedge fund's trades. Thus, it may very well be that having cash lenders fund dealers who in turn fund their clients is an efficient outcome. This is an important question for future research.

References

Adrian, T., Begalle, B., Copeland, A. and Martin, A. (2013), Repo and securities lending, *in* 'Risk Topography: Systemic Risk and Macro Modeling', University of Chicago Press.

Bottazzi, J.-M., Luque, J. and Páscoa, M. R. (2012), 'Securities market theory: Possession, repo and rehypothecation', *Journal of Economic Theory* **147**(2), 477–500.

Brunnermeier, M. and Pedersen, L. (2009), 'Market liquidity and funding liquidity', *Review of Financial studies* **22**(6), 2201–2238.

Copeland, A., Davis, I., LeSueur, E. and Martin, A. (2012), 'Mapping and sizing the U.S. repo market', *Federal Reserve Bank of New York Liberty Street Economics blog, June* **25**.

Copeland, A., Martin, A. and Walker, M. (2014), 'Repo runs: evidence from the tri-party repo market', *The Journal of Finance* **69**(6), 2343–2380.

Duffie, D. (2013), 'Replumbing our financial system: Uneven progress', *International Journal of Central Banking* **9**(1), 251–279.

Duffie, D., Garleanu, N. and Pedersen, L. H. (2002), 'Securities lending, shorting, and pricing', *Journal of Financial Economics* **66**(2), 307–339.

Eren, E. (2014), 'Intermediary funding liquidity and rehypothecation as a determinant of repo haircuts and interest rates', *working paper, Stanford University* .

Fleming, M. J. and Garbade, K. (2003), 'The repurchase agreement refined: GCF repo', *Current Issues in Economics and Finance* **9**(6).

Fostel, A. and Geanakoplos, J. (2011), 'Endogenous leverage: VaR and beyond', *Cowles Foundation for Research in Economics, Yale University* .

Geanakoplos, J. (2010), 'The Leverage Cycle', *NBER Macroeconomics Annual 2009* **24**, 1–65.

Gorton, G. and Metrick, A. (2012), 'Securitized banking and the run on repo', *Journal of Financial Economics* **104**(3), 425–451.

Infante, S. (2013), 'Screening through margins: A model of repo lending', *working paper, Federal Reserve Board* .

Krishnamurthy, A., Nagel, S. and Orlov, D. (2014), 'Sizing up repo', *The Journal of Finance* **69**(6), 2381–2417.

Martin, A., Skeie, D. and Von Thadden, E.-L. (2014), 'Repo runs', *Review of Financial Studies* **27**(4), 957–989.

Mitchell, M. and Pulvino, T. (2012), 'Arbitrage crashes and the speed of capital', *Journal of Financial Economics* **104**(3), 469–490.

Simsek, A. (2013), 'Belief disagreements and collateral constraints', *Econometrica* **81**(1), 1–53.

Singh, M. (2011), *Velocity of pledged collateral: analysis and implications*, International Monetary Fund.

A Appendix

Proof of Theorem 1:

The proof of the Theorem will consist in exploring equilibria that separate each interaction of the intermediation and then puts the pieces together to characterize the final equilibrium.

Under general distribution assumptions, the intermediation problem's Lagrangean takes the following form:

$$
\begin{aligned}
\mathcal{L} &= \theta \log\left(\mathbb{E}\left(U^D\right) - v_0\right) + (1-\theta)\log\left(\hat{\mathbb{E}}\left(U^H\right) - W\right) + \mu_s(m^H - m^M) + \mu_b(m^H + F^H - (m^M + F^M)) \\
&\quad + \mu_m(W - m^H) + \mu\left(pu^M(F^M) + (1-p)\left[u^M(F^M)(1 - G(F^M|i)) + \int_{\underline{a}}^{F^M} u^M(\eta)dG(\eta|i)\right] - u^M(a - m^M)\right)
\end{aligned}
$$

Taking FOC gives:

$$
\frac{\partial \mathcal{L}}{\partial m^H} = \left(\frac{\theta}{\mathbb{E}\left(U^D\right) - v_0}\right)\frac{\partial \mathbb{E}\left(U^D\right)}{\partial m^H} + \left(\frac{1-\theta}{\mathbb{E}\left(U^H\right) - W}\right)\frac{\partial \mathbb{E}\left(U^H\right)}{\partial m^H} + \mu_s + \mu_b - \mu_m \leq 0 \tag{4}
$$

$$
\frac{\partial \mathcal{L}}{\partial F^H} = \left(\frac{\theta}{\mathbb{E}\left(U^D\right) - v_0}\right)\frac{\partial \mathbb{E}\left(U^D\right)}{\partial F^H} + \left(\frac{1-\theta}{\mathbb{E}\left(U^H\right) - W}\right)\frac{\partial \mathbb{E}\left(U^H\right)}{\partial F^H} + \mu_b \leq 0 \tag{5}
$$

$$
\frac{\partial \mathcal{L}}{\partial m^M} = \left(\frac{\theta}{\mathbb{E}\left(U^D\right) - v_0}\right)\frac{\partial \mathbb{E}\left(U^D\right)}{\partial m^M} + \mu u^{M'}(a - m^M) - \mu_s - \mu_b \leq 0 \tag{6}
$$

$$
\frac{\partial \mathcal{L}}{\partial F^M} = \left(\frac{\theta}{\mathbb{E}\left(U^D\right) - v_0}\right)\frac{\partial \mathbb{E}\left(U^D\right)}{\partial F^M} + \mu[p + (1-p)(1 - G(F^M))]u^{M'}(F^M) - \mu_b \leq 0 \tag{7}
$$

where

$$
\frac{\partial \mathbb{E}\left(U^D\right)}{\partial m^H} = v'(m^H - m^M) - G(m^H + F^H - W|s)
$$

$$
\frac{\partial \mathbb{E}\left(U^D\right)}{\partial F^H} = 1 - G(m^H + F^H - W|s)
$$

$$
\frac{\partial \mathbb{E}\left(U^D\right)}{\partial m^M} = -v'(m^H - m^M)
$$

$$
\frac{\partial \mathbb{E}\left(U^D\right)}{\partial F^M} = -1
$$

$$
\frac{\partial \hat{\mathbb{E}}\left(U^H\right)}{\partial m^H} = -(1 - \hat{G}(m^H + F^H - W))
$$

$$
\frac{\partial \hat{\mathbb{E}}\left(U^H\right)}{\partial F^H} = -p(1 - \hat{G}(m^H + F^H - W)|s) - (1-p)(\hat{G}(F^H|i) - \hat{G}(m^H + F^H - W|i))
$$

Given that I consider the case where $\tilde{a}$ only has two outcomes $\{\bar{a}, \underline{a}\}$, I have to consider "kinks" in the payoff function. Specifically, in the dealer-HF case when $m^H + F^H \vee W + \underline{a}$ and $F^H \vee \underline{a}$, and in the dealer-MMF case when $F^M \vee \underline{a}$. Whenever the contracts are risky (i.e., either hedge fund or money fund can suffer a loss), I add a multiplier μ_{Ri} to the corresponding FOC, and whenever they are safe I subtract a multiplier μ_{Si} to the corresponding FOC; where i denotes which counterparty under consideration. This will affect equations (4) and (5) when dealing with a risky or safe dealer-HF contract, and equation (7) when dealing with a risky or safe dealer-MMF contract. The additional kink in F for dealer-HF problem will have a multiplier $\bar{\mu}_F$ or $\underline{\mu}_F$, which will only affects equation (5).

Note that if the self financing conditions aren't active, then there is no connection – other than the Dealers expected payoff – that relates the dealer-HF problem with the dealer-MMF problem. In this version of the paper, I shall focus on the separable case and drop the self financing multipliers when necessary. Also, I shall only consider optimal contracts where the upper bound on m^H is slack, i.e., $m^H < W$.

Dealer-MMF Problem (D-MMF):

In the case where the outcome of the asset is binary, and assuming $m^M, F^M > 0$, equations (6) and (7) are reduced to,

$$\left(\frac{-\theta v'(m^H - m^M)}{\mathbb{E}(U^D) - v_0}\right) + \mu u^{M'}(a - m^M) - \mu_s - \mu_b = 0$$

$$\left(-\frac{\theta}{\mathbb{E}(U^D) - v_0}\right) + \mu[p + (1-p)(1 - G(F^M|i))]u^{M'}(F^M) - \mu_b = 0.$$

where $1 - G(F^M) = \alpha$ if $F^M \geq \underline{a}$ and 1 if $F^M \leq \underline{a}$. Thus, there are two cases to analyze: F^M greater or less than $\underline{a}$.

(D-MMF) Case I – $F^M \geq \underline{a}$: Solving for μ from the first equation gives,

$$\mu = \frac{1}{u^{M'}(a - m^M)}\left[\left(\frac{\theta v'(m^H - m^M)}{\mathbb{E}(U^D) - v_0}\right) + \mu_s + \mu_b\right] > 0$$

Replacing that expression for μ in equation (7) gives,

$$0 = \left(\frac{\theta}{\mathbb{E}(U^D) - v_0}\right)\left[v'(m^H - m^M)\frac{u^{M'}(F^M)}{u^{M'}(a - m^M)}[1 - (1-\alpha)(1-\rho)] - 1\right]$$
$$+ \mu_b \underbrace{\left[\frac{u^{M'}(F^M)}{u^{M'}(a - m^M)}[1 - (1-\alpha)(1-\rho)] - 1\right]}_{<0} + \mu_s \frac{u^{M'}(F^M)}{u^{M'}(a - m^M)}[1 - (1-\alpha)(1-\rho)] + \mu_{RM}$$

Because $F^M \geq a - m^M$, only the first "large bracket term" may be zero if the Dealer's marginal payoff for cash today is relatively large.

Assuming the self financing conditions do not bind ($\mu_s = \mu_b = 0$), there exist two possible solutions: a risk free and risky outcome.

(D-MMF) Case I.1 – Safe Outcome $F^M = \underline{a}, m^M = a - \underline{a}$, implying $u^{M'}(F^M) = u^{M'}(a - m^M)$, which gives,

$$\mu_{RM} = \left(\frac{\theta}{\mathbb{E}(U^D) - v_0}\right)\underbrace{\left(1 - v'(m^H - m^M)[1 - (1-\alpha)(1-\rho)]\right)}_{\vee 0?}$$

thus μ_{RM} is positive if and only if $1 > v'(m^H - m^M)[1 - (1-\alpha)(1-\rho)]$. Condition i) and iii) gives $v' < \frac{1}{1 - (1-\alpha)(1-\rho)}$. Intuitively the upside of additional cash today cannot outweigh the additional compensation for the MMF's extra risk.

(D-MMF) Case I.2 – Risky Outcome $F^M > \underline{a}, m^M$ solving MMF's IR, implying $u^{M'}(F^M) < u^{M'}(a - m^M)$ and $\mu_{RM} = 0$, which gives,

$$0 = \left(\frac{\theta}{\mathbb{E}(U^D) - v_0}\right)\left(v'(m^H - m^M)\frac{u^{M'}(F^M)}{u^{M'}(a - m^M)}[1 - (1-\alpha)(1-\rho)] - 1\right)$$

and only occurs if the "large bracket term is zero". For this version of the paper, I shall only focus on safe dealer money market contracts.

(D-MMF) Case II – $F^M \leq \underline{a}$: For all of these cases, the IR constraint implies $u^M(a - m^M) = u^M(F^M)$. Solving for μ from (6) again gives,

$$\mu = \frac{1}{u^{M'}(a - m^M)}\left[\left(\frac{\theta v'(m^H - m^M)}{\mathbb{E}(U^D) - v_0}\right) + \mu_s + \mu_b\right] > 0$$

replacing back in equation (7) now gives,

$$0 = \underbrace{\left(\frac{\theta}{\mathbb{E}(U^D) - v_0}\right)\left[v'(m^H - m^M) - 1\right]}_{>0} + \mu_s - \mu_{SM}$$

Therefore, if we assume that the self financing conditions do not bind ($\mu_s = 0$), there exist only one solution (since $v'(\cdot) > 1$): $F^M = \underline{a}$ and $m^M = a - \underline{a}$. The intuition is that when the repo is risk free, the MMF is indifferent between m^M and F^M, making the dealer's preference for cash today dominate, and thus pushing up the final debt payment.

Dealer-HF Problem (D-HF):

The more interesting problem comes from analyzing the interaction between the Dealer and HF. Assuming that the decision variables are positive, $m^M, F^M > 0$, equations (4) and (5) are reduced to,

$$\left(\frac{\theta(v'(m^H - m^M) - G(m^H + F^H - W|s))}{\mathbb{E}\left(U^D\right) - v_0}\right) - \left(\frac{(1-\theta)(1 - \hat{G}(m^H + F^H - W))}{\mathbb{E}\left(U^H\right) - W}\right)$$
$$+ \mu_s + \mu_b = 0$$

$$-\left(\frac{(1-\theta)(p(1 - \hat{G}(m^H + F^H - W|s)) + (1-p)(\hat{G}(F^H|i) - \hat{G}(m^H + F^H - W|i)))}{\mathbb{E}\left(U^H\right) - W}\right)$$
$$+ \left(\frac{\theta(1 - G(m^H + F^H - W|s))}{\mathbb{E}\left(U^D\right) - v_0}\right) + \mu_b = 0 \qquad (8)$$

Note that replacing the second equation in the first gives the following condition,

$$\left(\frac{\theta(v'(m^H - m^M) - 1)}{\mathbb{E}\left(U^D\right) - v_0}\right) - \left(\frac{(1-\theta)(1-p)(1 - \hat{G}(F^H|i))}{\mathbb{E}\left(U^H\right) - W}\right) + \mu_s = 0 \qquad (9)$$

Under a binary asset payoff, HF's optimism is reduced to $\hat{\alpha} > \alpha$; and there are three cases to consider: $\underline{a} + W \vee m^H + F^H$ and $\underline{a} \vee F^H$.[22] Note that given that HF optimism is with respect to the payoff probability and not the level of payoffs, the thresholds are the same for the dealer and HF. Moreover, note that the safe and risky multiplier μ_{RH}, μ_{SH} enter the FOC for m^H and F^H, therefore they cancel out when deriving equation (9).[23] But the same cannot be said about $\bar{\mu}_F$ and $\underline{\mu}_F$ which appears in equation (9) with the sign changed from the original FOC equation.

Case I $- m^H + F^H \geq \underline{a} + W$: In this case, the reduced FOC translate to,

$$\left(\frac{\theta(v'(m^H - m^M) - 1)}{\mathbb{E}\left(U^D\right) - v_0}\right) - \left(\frac{(1-\theta)((1-p) - (1-\hat{\alpha})(1-\rho))}{\mathbb{E}\left(U^H\right) - W}\right) + \mu_s = 0$$

$$\left(\frac{\theta\left(1 - \frac{\rho(1-\alpha)}{p}\right)}{\mathbb{E}\left(U^D\right) - v_0}\right) - \left(\frac{(1-\theta)p\left(1 - \frac{\rho(1-\hat{\alpha})}{p}\right)}{\mathbb{E}\left(U^H\right) - W}\right) + \mu_b + \mu_{RH} = 0$$

(D-HF) Case I.1 $- m^H + F^H > \underline{a} + W$: Assume that the self financing conditions do not bind ($\mu_s = \mu_b = 0$) and that the risky threshold is slack; the above equations can two different expressions for $\frac{(1-\theta)(\mathbb{E}(U^D) - v_0)}{\theta(\mathbb{E}(U^H) - W)}$. Equalizing these expressions gives,

$$\frac{pv'(m^H - m^M) - \rho(1-\alpha)}{p - \rho(1-\alpha)} = \frac{\hat{\alpha}}{p - \rho(1-\hat{\alpha})}$$

which is equation (2). Note that this expression only depends on m^H and m^M, that is, final repayments are irrelevant. Intuitively, it trades off the cost borne by the HF due to the dealer's default and the dealer's preference for cash today, equalizing both players marginal rate of substitution between m^H and F^H. Rearranging terms gives $v' = \frac{\hat{\alpha}}{p}\left\{\frac{p - \rho(1-\alpha)}{p - \rho(1-\hat{\alpha})}\right\} + \frac{\rho}{p}(1-\alpha)$. Having a condition for m^H, in this case the equation to solve for F^H is given by,

$$F^H = \theta F_{MonoD} + (1-\theta)F_{MonoH}$$

where F_{MonoD} is the dealer's monopolist solution (i.e., making the HF break even) and F_{MonoH} is the HF's monopolist solution

---

[22] Note that $\underline{a} + W - m^H > \underline{a}$.
[23] Just like μ_b.

(i.e., making the dealer break even). In effect, with a risky contract the firms' payoffs are given by,

$$\mathbb{E}\left(U^D\right) - v_0 = v(m^H - m^M) - v_0 + \left(\left(1 - \frac{\rho(1-\alpha)}{p}\right)F^H + \frac{\rho(1-\alpha)}{p}(\underline{a} + W - m^H) - F^M\right)$$

$$\mathbb{E}\left(U^H\right) - W = p\left(1 - \frac{\rho(1-\hat{\alpha})}{p}\right)(\overline{a} + W - m^H - F^H) + (1-p)\left(1 - \frac{(1-\rho)(1-\hat{\alpha})}{1-p}\right)(W - m) - W$$

note F^H appears linearly in both expressions, thus we can separate them in terms grouped by θ and $1-\theta$. In that case, the Dealer's payoff evaluated in F^H_{MonoH} is zero and the HF's payoff valuated in F^H_{MonoD} is zero. Finally, using expression for the ratio between payoffs which doesn't involve the Dealer's preference for cash today v, resulting in,

$$p\left(1 - \frac{\rho(1-\hat{\alpha})}{p}\right)(1-\theta)\left(\mathbb{E}\left(U^D\right) - v_0\right) = \left(1 - \frac{\rho(1-\alpha)}{p}\right)\theta(\mathbb{E}\left(U^H\right) - W)$$

where, conditional on being a risky contract, the utility functions are linear. Swapping F_{MonoD} with F_{MonoH} which are pre multiplied by $p\left(1 - \frac{\rho(1-\hat{\alpha})}{p}\right)(1-\theta)$ and $\left(1 - \frac{\rho(1-\alpha)}{p}\right)\theta$ respectively, gives the original expression of each agents payoff so that they break even, implying the solution in fact does solve the FOC's.

Finally, to ensure that this in fact is a solution, it's necessary to verify that in fact $F^H > \underline{a} + W - m^H$. Each sub expression of F^H takes the following form,

$$F_{MonoD} = \overline{a} - \frac{((1-\hat{\alpha})W + \hat{\alpha}m^H)}{p - \rho(1-\hat{\alpha})}$$

$$F_{MonoH} = \frac{v_0 - v(m^H - m^M) - \frac{\rho(1-\alpha)}{p}(\underline{a} + W - m^H) + F^M}{\left(1 - \frac{\rho(1-\alpha)}{p}\right)}$$

Note that F_{MonoD} will satisfy the condition if $p(\hat{a} - \underline{a}) > W(p\hat{\alpha} + (1-\hat{\alpha})) + (1-p)\hat{\alpha}m^H$, since F_{MonoD} is decreasing in ρ and $\rho \leq p$. [24] That is, the HF's optimism has to be high enough for it to assume the loss in case of default. Therefore if the Dealer has significant market power, then the weighted average can be above the threshold.

(D-HF) Case I.2– $m^H + F^H = \underline{a} + W$: Assume that the self financing conditions do not bind ($\mu_s = \mu_b = 0$) and that the risky threshold binds. Therefore we have the following equations,

$$\frac{(1-\theta)\left(\mathbb{E}\left(U^D\right) - v_0\right)}{\theta(\mathbb{E}\left(U^H\right) - W)} = \frac{(v'(m^H - m^M) - 1)}{(1-p) - (1-\rho)(1-\hat{\alpha})}$$

$$\frac{(1-\theta)\left(\mathbb{E}\left(U^D\right) - v_0\right)}{\theta(\mathbb{E}\left(U^H\right) - W)} - \frac{(p - \rho(1-\alpha))}{p(p - \rho(1-\hat{\alpha}))} = \hat{\mu}_{RH}.$$

For this to be a solution it's necessary to have, $\frac{p(v'-1)}{(1-p)-(1-\rho)(1-\hat{\alpha})} > \frac{p - \rho(1-\alpha)}{p - \rho(1-\hat{\alpha})}$. This proposed equilibrium would have $m^H + F^H = \underline{a} + W$.

(D-HF) Case II – $F^H \in [\underline{a}, \underline{a} + W - m^H]$: In this case, the reduced FOC translate to,

$$\left(\frac{\theta(v'(m^H - m^M) - 1)}{\mathbb{E}\left(U^D\right) - v_0}\right) - \left(\frac{(1-\theta)((1-p) - (1-\hat{\alpha})(1-\rho))}{\mathbb{E}\left(U^H\right) - W}\right) + \mu_s - \overline{\mu}_F = 0$$

$$\left(\frac{\theta}{\mathbb{E}\left(U^D\right) - v_0}\right) - \left(\frac{(1-\theta)(p + (1-\hat{\alpha})(1-\rho))}{\mathbb{E}\left(U^H\right) - W}\right) + \mu_b - \mu_{SH} = 0$$

(D-HF) Case II.1 – $F^H \in (\underline{a}, \underline{a} + W - m^H)$: Assume that the self financing conditions do not bind ($\mu_s = \mu_b = 0$) and that repurchase price restrictions are slack. The original FOC equations give two different expressions for $\frac{(1-\theta)\left(\mathbb{E}\left(U^D\right) - v_0\right)}{\theta(\mathbb{E}\left(U^H\right) - W)}$.

---

[24]Note that since $W > m^H$, the condition $p(\hat{a} - \underline{a}) > W$ is enough to ensure the above occurs.

Equalizing these expressions gives,

$$\frac{v'(m^H - m^M) - 1}{(1-p) - (1-\hat{\alpha})(1-\rho)} = \frac{1}{p + (1-\hat{\alpha})(1-\rho)}. \tag{10}$$

Rearranging equation (10) gives $v' = \frac{1}{p+(1-\hat{\alpha})(1-\rho)}$. Note that this expression only depends on m^H and m^M, that is, final repayments are irrelevant. Having a condition for m^H, in this case the equation to solve for F^H is given by,

$$F^H = \theta F_{MonoD} + (1-\theta) F_{MonoH}$$

where F_{MonoD} is the Dealer's monopolist solution (i.e., making the HF break even) and F_{MonoH} is the HF's monopolist solution (i.e., making the Dealer break even). In effect, with $F^H \in (\underline{a}, \underline{a} + W - m^H)$ the firms' payoffs are given by,

$$\mathbb{E}\left(U^D\right) - v_0 = v(m^H - m^M) - v_0 + F^H - F^M$$
$$\mathbb{E}\left(U^H\right) - W = (p - \rho(1-\hat{\alpha}))\bar{a} + (1-\hat{\alpha})\underline{a} - (p + (1-\hat{\alpha})(1-\rho))F^H - m^H.$$

F^H appears linearly in both expressions, thus we can separate them in terms grouped by θ and $1-\theta$. In that case, the Dealer's payoff evaluated in F_{MonoH} is zero and the HF's payoff valuated in F_{MonoD} is zero. Evaluating F^H in the expression involving the ratio of excess payoffs verifies that the conjectured repurchase price satisfies the FOC's.

To ensure that this in fact is a solution, it's necessary to verify that in fact $F^H \in (\underline{a}, \underline{a} + W - m^H)$. Each sub expression of F^H takes the following form,

$$F_{MonoD} = \frac{(p - \rho(1-\hat{\alpha}))\bar{a} + (1-\hat{\alpha})\underline{a} - m^H}{p + (1-\hat{\alpha})(1-\rho)}$$
$$F_{MonoH} = v_0 - v(m^H - m^M) + F^M.$$

(D-HF) Case II.2 – $F^H = \underline{a} + W - m^H$: Assume that the self financing conditions do not bind ($\mu_s = \mu_b = 0$) the optimal contract is marginally safe. The first equation of this case gives an expression for $\frac{(1-\theta)(\mathbb{E}(U^D) - v_0)}{\theta(\mathbb{E}(U^H) - W)}$, which included in the second FOC equation implies,

$$\frac{1}{p + (1-\hat{\alpha})(1-\rho)} - \frac{(v'(m^H - m^M) - 1)}{(1-p) - (1-\hat{\alpha})(1-\rho)} = \hat{\mu}_{SH}$$

Therefore this solution is optimal in this case when $\frac{1}{p+(1-\hat{\alpha})(1-\rho)} > \frac{(v'-1)}{(1-p)-(1-\hat{\alpha})(1-\rho)}$. The proposed equilibrium would have $F^{H*} + m^{H*} = \underline{a} + W$ and m^{H*} would be pinned down by the ratio of excess payoffs equal to $\frac{v'(m^{H*} - m^M) - 1}{(1-p) - (1-\hat{\alpha})(1-\rho)}$.

(D-HF) Case II.3 – $F^H = \underline{a}$: Assume that the self financing conditions do not bind ($\mu_s = \mu_b = 0$) and that the threshold on F^H binds. The second equation of this case gives an expression for $\frac{(1-\theta)(\mathbb{E}(U^D) - v_0)}{\theta(\mathbb{E}(U^H) - W)}$, which included in the first FOC equation implies,

$$\frac{v'(m^H - m^M) - 1}{(1-p) - (1-\hat{\alpha})(1-\rho)} - \frac{1}{p + (1-\hat{\alpha})(1-\rho)} = \hat{\hat{\mu}}_F$$

Therefore this solution is optimal in this case when $\frac{v'-1}{(1-p)-(1-\hat{\alpha})(1-\rho)} > \frac{1}{p+(1-\hat{\alpha})(1-\rho)}$. This proposed equilibrium would have $F^{H*} = \underline{a}$, and m^{H*} would be pinned down by the ratio of excess payoffs equal to $\frac{1}{p+(1-\hat{\alpha})(1-\rho)}$.

(D-HF) Case III – $F^H \leq \underline{a}$: In this case, the reduced FOC translate to,

$$\left(\frac{\theta(v'(m^H - m^M) - 1)}{\mathbb{E}(U^D) - v_0}\right) - \left(\frac{(1-\theta)(1-p)}{\mathbb{E}(U^H) - W}\right) + \mu_s + \underline{\mu}_F = 0$$
$$\left(\frac{\theta}{\mathbb{E}(U^D) - v_0}\right) - \left(\frac{(1-\theta)p}{\mathbb{E}(U^H) - W}\right) + \mu_b = 0$$

(D-HF) Case III.1 – $F^H < \underline{a}$: Assume that the self financing conditions do not bind ($\mu_s = \mu_b = 0$) and that repurchase price restriction is slack. The original FOC equations give two different expressions for $\frac{(1-\theta)(\mathbb{E}(U^D) - v_0)}{\theta(\mathbb{E}(U^H) - W)}$. Equalizing these expressions gives,

$$v'(m^H - m^M) - 1 = \frac{(1-p)}{p}$$

Note that this expression only depends on m^H and m^M, that is, final repayments are irrelevant. Having a condition for m^H, in this case the equation to solve for F^H is given by,

$$F^H = \theta F_{MonoD} + (1 - \theta) F_{MonoH}$$

where F_{MonoD} is the Dealer's monopolist solution (i.e., making the HF break even) and F_{MonoH} is the HF's monopolist solution (i.e., making the Dealer break even). In effect, with a safe contract the firms' payoffs are given by,

$$
\begin{aligned}
\mathbb{E}\left(U^D\right) - v_0 &= v(m^H - m^M) - v_0 + F^H - F^M \\
\mathbb{E}\left(U^H\right) - W &= p(\hat{a} - F^H) - m^H.
\end{aligned}
$$

Note F^H appears linearly in both expressions, thus we can separate them in terms grouped by θ and $1 - \theta$. In that case, the Dealer's payoff evaluated in F_{MonoH} is zero and the HF's payoff valuated in F_{MonoD} is zero. Evaluating F^H in the expression involving the ratio of excess payoffs verifies that this repurchase price satisfies the FOC's.

To ensure that this in fact is a solution, it's necessary to verify that in fact $F^H < \underline{a}$. Each sub expression of F^H takes the following form,

$$
\begin{aligned}
F_{MonoD} &= \hat{a} - \frac{m^H}{p} \\
F_{MonoH} &= v_0 - v(m^H - m^M) + F^M
\end{aligned}
$$

in this case it would be difficult to have the Dealer's monopolist solution satisfy the bound. In effect, one would need $\hat{a} - \frac{(1-p)m^H}{p} < \underline{a} + W$, which would be unlikely considering $m^H < W$. The case for the HF's monopolist solution with the MMF's safe solution (i.e., $F^M = \underline{a}$) then $F^H_{MH} = v_0 - v(m^H - m^M) + \underline{a} < \underline{a} + W - m^H$ always holds. In this case, the solution satisfies the condition if the HF has relatively more market power. Note that it would also need to be verified that the self financing conditions hold, but I shall leave that analysis for when I consider both solutions in conjunction.

(D-HF) Case III.2– $F^H = \underline{a}$: Assume that the self financing conditions do not bind ($\mu_s = \mu_b = 0$) and that the threshold on F^H binds. Therefore we have the following equations,

$$
\begin{aligned}
\left(\frac{(1-\theta)(\mathbb{E}\left(U^D\right) - v_0)}{\theta(\mathbb{E}\left(U^H\right) - W)}\right) - \left(\frac{v'(m^H - m^M) - 1}{(1-p)}\right) &= \hat{\underline{\mu}}_F \\
\left(\frac{(1-\theta)(\mathbb{E}\left(U^D\right) - v_0)}{\theta(\mathbb{E}\left(U^H\right) - W)}\right) &= \frac{1}{p}
\end{aligned}
$$

therefore for this to be an equilibrium $\frac{1-p}{p} > v'(m^H - m^M) - 1$. This proposed equilibrium would have $F^H = \underline{a}$ and m^{H*} would be pinned down by the ratio of excess payoffs equal to $1/p$.

Bringing the Dealer-HF Problem & Dealer-MMF Problem:

The proposed safe solution in the Dealer-MMF is in fact an equilibrium iff:

$$v'(m^H - m^M) \in \left(1, \frac{1}{1 - (1-\alpha)(1-\rho)}\right) \tag{11}$$

and any proposed solution of the Dealer-HF is in fact an equilibrium iff:

$$v'(m^H - m^M) \in \left[\frac{\hat{\alpha}}{p} \left\{ \frac{p - \rho(1-\alpha)}{p - \rho(1-\hat{\alpha})} \right\} + \frac{\rho}{p}(1-\alpha), \frac{1}{p} \right]$$

For a risky or marginal safe solution to in fact exist[25], I need to impose:

$$\frac{\hat{\alpha}}{p} \left\{ \frac{p - \rho(1-\alpha)}{p - \rho(1-\hat{\alpha})} \right\} + \frac{\rho}{p}(1-\alpha) < \frac{1}{1 - (1-\alpha)(1-\rho)}$$

which is condition i).

Thus under this parameterization, for a high enough θ, given assumption $ii)$ the optimal contract, with m^H equalizing the marginal rates of substitution characterized in equation (2):

$$\frac{pv'(m^H - (a - \underline{a})) - \rho(1-\alpha)}{p - \rho(1-\alpha)} = \frac{\hat{\alpha}}{p - \rho(1-\hat{\alpha})}$$

and F^H close to the dealer's monopolist repurchase price, leading to a hedge fund default in case of a bad asset outcome. This is Case I.1 in the Dealer-HF problem and results in feasible $m \leq W$ due to assumption iii).

To keep the analysis simple, the Theorem only characterized equilibria where the MMF has a riskless contract and that at best, the hedge fund has a risky contract or marginally safe contract. The latter occurs whenever $m^H + F^H = \underline{a} + W$, which is Case II.2. For θ close to 1, the equilibrium is characterized by Case I.1. As θ decreases, the repurchase price falls till the optimal contract becomes riskless (i.e., $\underline{a} + W = m^H + F^H$), which occurs whenever $\theta = \theta^S$. Then, the equilibrium is characterized by Case II.2, where the margin is pinned down by,

$$\frac{(1-\theta)\left(\mathbb{E}\left(U^D\right) - v_0\right)}{\theta(\mathbb{E}\left(U^H\right) - W)} = \frac{v' - 1}{(1-p) - (1-\hat{\alpha})(1-\rho)} \tag{12}$$

with $F^H = \underline{a} + W - m^H$.

As θ decrease the equilibrium characterized by equation (12) is sustained till one of the following conditions are met: Either the optimal m^H is low enough for the equilibrium to be characterized by Case II.1 (that is, whenever $\frac{v'-1}{(1-p)-(1-\hat{\alpha})(1-\rho)} = \frac{1}{p+(1-\hat{\alpha})(1-\rho)}$), or the optimal m^H implies a risky MMF contract (that is, $v' \geq \frac{1}{1-(1-\alpha)(1-\rho)}$). The lower bound $\underline{\theta}$ is defined as the minimum θ such that both these conditions are met. Thus, the Theorem has two equilibrium characterizations: one for for $\theta \in (\underline{\theta}, \theta^S]$ given by Case I.1 and another for $\theta \in [\theta^S, 1)$ given by Case II.2.

∎

Proof of Proposition 1: The result stems by taking the implicit derivative of the equilibrium conditions when $\theta = \underline{\theta}$. Recall that $\underline{\theta}$ is defined as the smallest value of θ such that a riskless money market solution is possible, i.e.,

$$\frac{v'(m^H - m^M) - 1}{1 - p} = \frac{1 - \alpha}{p + (1-p)\alpha}.$$

For this value of θ the equilibrium is characterized by $m^H + F^H = W + \underline{a}$ and

$$\frac{(1-\underline{\theta})\left(\mathbb{E}\left(U^D\right) - v_0\right)}{\underline{\theta}(\mathbb{E}\left(U^H\right) - W)} = \frac{v'(m^{H*} - m^{M*}) - 1}{\hat{\alpha}(1-p)}.$$

giving the following equality:

$$\hat{\alpha}(1-\underline{\theta})(p + (1-p)\alpha)\left(\mathbb{E}\left(U^D\right) - v_0\right) = \underline{\theta}(1-\alpha)\left(\mathbb{E}\left(U^H\right) - W\right).$$

---

[25]Where "marginal safe" implies that $m^H + F^H = \underline{a} + W$

32

First, considering the original model and deriving with respect to p gives,

$$\frac{\partial \underline{\theta}}{\partial p}\left[(p + (1-p)\alpha)(\mathbb{E}(U^D) - v_0) + (1-\alpha)(\mathbb{E}(U^H) - W)\right] = \hat{\alpha}(1-\underline{\theta})(1-\alpha)(\mathbb{E}(U^D) - v_0) - \underline{\theta}(1-\alpha)\frac{\partial(\mathbb{E}(U^H) - W)}{\partial p} +$$

$$\left[\hat{\alpha}(1-\underline{\theta})(p + (1-p)\alpha)(v'(m^H - m^M) - 1) + \underline{\theta}(1-\alpha)(1-p)\hat{\alpha}\right]\frac{\partial m}{\partial p}.$$

Note that due to the equilibrium condition $(p + (1-p)\alpha)(v'(m^H - m^M) - 1) = (1-\alpha)(1-p)$. Also, given that in this equilibrium, the optimal dealer hedge fund contract is safe, $\frac{\partial(\mathbb{E}(U^H) - W)}{\partial p} = \hat{\alpha}(\overline{a} - F^H)$, therefore,

$$\frac{\partial(\mathbb{E}(U^H) - W)}{\partial p} = \left(\mathbb{E}(U^H) - W)\right) + \underbrace{(1-p)\hat{\alpha}(\overline{a} - F^H) + m^H - (1-\hat{\alpha})(\underline{a} - F^H)}_{:=\Gamma > 0}.$$

Using these last two observations to solve for the partial derivative of $\underline{\theta}$,

$$\frac{\partial \underline{\theta}}{\partial p} = \frac{\hat{\alpha}(1-\underline{\theta})(1-\alpha)(\mathbb{E}(U^D) - v_0) - \underline{\theta}(1-\alpha)(\mathbb{E}(U^H) - W) - \Gamma + (1-\alpha)(1-p)\frac{\partial m}{\partial p}}{[(p + (1-p)\alpha)(\mathbb{E}(U^D) - v_0) + (1-\alpha)(\mathbb{E}(U^H) - W)]}.$$

Note that $\hat{\alpha}(1-\underline{\theta})(1-\alpha)(\mathbb{E}(U^D) - v_0) - \underline{\theta}(1-\alpha)(\mathbb{E}(U^H) - W) < 0$ for p sufficiently large, given the initial equation to pin down $\underline{\theta}$. Therefore, a p sufficiently close to 1 implies $\frac{\partial \underline{\theta}}{\partial p} < 0$.

■

www.ingramcontent.com/pod-product-compliance
Lightning Source LLC
Chambersburg PA
CBHW080623180526
45168CB00007B/3037